T0368595

Five Golden Years

Brooklyn 5.0

LINDA BERRY

BOOK 5 OF 5

Copyright © 2024 by Linda Berry. 863396

All rights reserved. No part of this book may be reproduced
or transmitted in any form or by any means, electronic
or mechanical, including photocopying, recording, or
by any information storage and retrieval system, without
permission in writing from the copyright owner.

To order additional copies of this book, contact:
Xlibris
844-714-8691
www.Xlibris.com
Orders@Xlibris.com

ISBN: Softcover   979-8-3694-3374-4
        EBook   979-8-3694-3208-2

Print information available on the last page

Rev. date: 11/12/2024

Table of Contents

Introduction

Book 5 brings together the child mentally, cognitively, physically, intellectually diabolically and metaphysically. When Brooklyn was one year old, she could sing happy birthday with no help and place a name in the right place. This skill magnifies unselfishness by recognizing that you are not the center of attraction all the time. That is why the first book was called the magnificent one. It's magical to hear her pronounce words clearly. By the age of two Brooklyn was in a full routine of going to the learning factory and accepting the full routine of following the nightly parental rules of bathing, preparing for bed, waking up and getting ready to learn. Age three brought about another level of learning which personifies defendant cognitive skills that can be learned by all ages. Most preschoolers start coloring and recognizing words. These students are writing letters and reading words. Thus, the book level three evolved. The facilitator Nana Wynn can work with students whether they have a developmental disability or an unusual cognitive learning start. Some parents feel the educational system is not within them to help their child. The difference is this class has homework so family and friends can enjoy extending the learning curb. Beyond school a child learns who their family members are. Book four introduces the family and Brooklyn's sibling Willow. She understands who her parents and grandparents are. Putting the name Aunt and Uncle in front of a name signifies a relationship. Book five pulls it all together. One summer when went to her family reunion in Texas, she performed on stage by singing.

When the people clapped, she gladly accepted their gratitude. At this point confidence has sat in. When a child understands sharing toys, or food that is one part. Being friendly and having manners no matter where you go is commendable. It reflects on the family upbringing as well. Now comes book five to show children celebrating holidays with family and friends is a part of growing up.

Skilled teachers, caregivers, universities, guardians, all parents who oversee children ages one through five will benefit from having this serious. It's fun, entertaining, educational, colorful, and lively.

In America there are international holidays celebrated everyday such as international hot-dog day, international cookie day, and something every day of the year. Let's see how one of Americas most famous loving family The Berry's celebrate good times on national holidays. From books one through five this series comes alive with the girl wonder Brooklyn who plays and thrives.

January

Happy New Year

Church offers services for all families who want to attend. In some homes, around 8 o'clock at night family, friends, cousins, and grandparents gather to eat and catch up with family news. Five minutes to 12 people start looking at tv to get the times square ball drop live on TV. The countdown begins, everyone gets their punch cups. It's time to countdown loud and all together; 10... 9...8...7...6...5...4...3......2...1!!!! Happy New Years says everyone as they hold their glasses in the air. Everyone is hugging, laughing and giving kisses. Cell phones are going off as well as people calling loved ones to wish them well. Long night, everyone gets to sleep in tomorrow. January 1 is the 1st holiday of the year.

Dr. Martin Luther King Jr's Day

For parents who work, the government will designate paid holidays off. Schools usually let children off on most of the same days. One holiday is Martin Luther King Jr's Birthday. This holiday is celebrated by attending local citywide programs. For example: In Columbus, Ohio, they have a Kings art center. Breakfast is provided, and many sub stations are set up to show the life a legacy of Dr. King. Children can color, music is playing, there are free give aways, dancing, performances and the like. They portray community service, social justice, and freedom themes. Brooklyn's dad fraternity, Alpha Phi Alpha, helped Contribute to the building of the MLK, Jr. monument.

Dad's Birthday

Boy oh boy oh boy!!!!! Owere all year mom, dad, family, and friends were invited to a local restaurant to celebrate dad's birthday. Food was ordered. People were taking pictures and talking and laughing all in honor of Brooklyn's dad. Some people brought presents; some people pinned money on him.

$\mathcal{F}$ebruary

Valentines Day

Valentine's Day is one of Ohio's lovely holidays. Workers. Daycare, pre-schools, and schools do not get this day off. People show love in many ways. Brooklyn's father has flowers for Brooklyn's mom. Everyone gets candy and a card. Brooklyn and her sister may get a surprise teddy bear. There are rose pebbles sprinkled everywhere. Love is in the air. Some students have a party in school or simply bring cards for the rest of the kids if is appropriate.

Presidents Day

This holiday is celebrated by looking at a lot of presidents and their history.

Fat Tuesday

Another day for Fat Tuesday is Mardi Gras. Mardi Gras is celebrated in New Orleans with parades. Fat Tuesday in Columbus, Ohio is celebrated by listening to jazz bands and eating. This holiday is celebrated by eating all the food you would like to eat. Food may be cooked, or families attend a special restaurant. One food item could be finding a prize in a cake or food item.

Lent

Lent begins the holy season. Some people call it Lent – Ash Wednesday. They may get ashes in the form of a cross on their forehead if time allows them to.

St. Patrick's Day

There is no day off for St. Patrick's Day. People do wear green all day and have parties. They eat corn beef, and drink green liquids.

Easter

This is the day the lord has made. Churches have a large group of participants. Children dress very well. The Saturday before Easter; Brooklyn's, mom, dad, aunts, uncles, and cousins gather for the large intense easter egg hunt. Golden eggs have money in them. The rest have candy and toys in them. The children are given baskets and off they go to the Easter egg hunt.

May

Mother's Day,

Nana Wynn helps the students make cards and gifts for their moms. One tradition is the fathers watch the kids, if that is the family choice. If your mom is living you may wear a red carnation. If your mom is not living a white carnation may be worn. When mothers go to church they get greeted with "Happy Mother's Day". Ladies receive flowers, cards, or candy all day. People exchange phone messages also for Mother's Day. If they go to dinner they may hear the same thing. People do stay at home to celebrate.

Memorial Day

By Memorial Day children are getting ready for the summer. The United States remember its fallen soldiers. One year Brooklyn and her family went to visit Grandma-Sita and Grandpa George. During her visit she was able to go to a nearby farm and see cows and touch them. In honor of Memorial Day, her Uncle Tommie was honored for his military service and his birthday. Everyone loves to eat cake and ice cream. Everyone ate, played and returned home.

June

Father's Day

The men of the family are celebrated by giving them a cookout in the back yard. The women cook the food. The children laugh and play. Overall, for the fathers, it's a fun day.

Juneteeth

Juneteeth is celebrated by having family and friends come over to taste cultured African American foods. Some of the foods consist of street corn, red fruits, green vegetables, deserts, assorted meats and snacks. When it gets dark all the guests go down the street to the school and watch fireworks displayed by Brooklyn male relatives.

July

 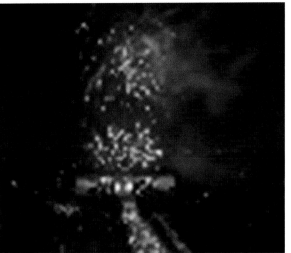

Independence Day

Independence Day is also called the 4th of July in America. Festivals, food, and fun. Some families celebrate at home. Some families have fun at beaches, and some families go on vacation. At the end of the day, most people look up in the sky to be graced with fireworks. Boom, pop, pop, bang, pow!!!!!!! Awwwwww exclaims the onlookers.

Moms Birthday

Oh! what a web to weave. Brooklyn's mom Ashley look soooooo…... beatified with her nails fancied, hair gussied up and attire fit to be admired. Ashley normally receives cards, gifts and phone calls for her birthday. She may be taken out and or celebrated with her husband, family and/or friends. It's her choice.

September

Labor Day,

Back to work, vacation is over, back to school, harvest the gardens its time to work!! There is no special order of the day. It may be celebrated by having the last hurrah with family and friends or by shopping for school and office supplies. There are many professionals in Brooklyn. One of those professionals is Brooklyn's Aunt Linda who she calls Auntie Peanut. Auntie Peanut is a chef. As a chef Linda must travel many places and complete many jobs.

Brookly's Birthday

This is my big day. It's my fifth birthday! By the time a child reaches five years old, they have reached a milestone. According to the Raising children network, academically a 5-year-old child can understand simple concepts like today, tomorrow, and yesterday. Not only can Brooklyn understand these concepts, but she can demonstrate them in sign language. A child can recognize seasons, and sight words and try to sound them out. Nana Wynn builds a binder with sight words in them and sends the binder home for her guardians to help with this task. Nana Wynn not only has her students see the words, pronounce, the words, but through leadership skills, read an appropriate book in front of the class. Intellectually a 5 year should be able to count to 10. Brooklyn was counting 40 snowballs at the raw age of two. A five-year-old should be able to understand the concept of food, and money, copy geometric shapes. Brooklyn mastered these skills, by having toys which allowed her to demonstrate these attributes. Through activities, a 5-year-old should be able to express emotion, make new friends, and play make believe games. Nana Wynn turned some games into cooking, voting, and the like. A five year should know that around 8:30pm its bedtime except for traveling away from home. In book two we learned that Brooklyn's bedtime manners include, a clean up song, to up all toys. Then upstairs for a fun bath. A story read by her parents and a bedtime prayer. Of course, each household is different. Overall, the child express independence, improved physical coordination, social play and more. One year the theme of Brooklyn's birthday party was going on a lion hunt. Her father was the lion, and the children invited to the event had lots of fun.

October

Sibling Willow Birthday

Birthdays in Brooklyn's household consist of themes. One year baby Willow birthday theme was a pumpkin fest. Children beheld a musical hayride and there were pumpkins all around the home. Who attends these parties. Parents with children. Grandparents, aunts, uncles, cousins and friends. Presents are not the only gifts given. Guest can place envelopes with contributions for colleges funds formally known as a 529 fund. Readers may think it's too early for such contributions but not the parents. They are smart as well as college graduates. They understand it's never too early to start saving for college.

Halloween

There is a park in Columbus, Ohio called Franklin Park Conservatory that hosts Princess, ferries, Ghost, goblins, candy and more. On this holiday, the community can bring children there to wear costumes and look at other youth. Some parents pass out candy, some guardians escort children to collect candy from home to home. At the end of the night, whoever oversees the children, checks the candy to make sure it is safe to eat. There are some households that host parties as well. Some neighborhoods have trick and trunk. In that case, the neighbors have treats in their trunks for the kids to enjoy. The first day after Halloween kicks off the holiday season. Cities start putting up Christmas decorations. Stores and organizations put up decorations and plan holiday parties as. It's the magical time of the year.

November

Veterans Day

Military members exist in Brooklyn's family. One of the youngest members is Brooklyn's uncle Tommie. Let's introduce some of Brooklyn's family members and how Veterans Day is celebrated. This is also the last day the flags are supposed to fly up at homes in the proper respect. Her Aunt Ebone' pronounced "Eb-o-nay" invited Uncle Tommie and Grandma Sita to her school because Tommie serves in the military serve in the Military. Granny-Sita retired from the military. At the time, Tommie was deployed to Afghanistan. Granny-Sita was able to reach him, and he spoke to the class by video phone. Ebone has three articulate, intelligent and beautiful children: Laila, Kalee, and Alex. One year these wonderful children made a patriot video for both. Other times, the twins, Kalee and Alex invited the two-family veterans to their school. There was one year when Brooklyn's Nana and family invited Granny-Sita and her comrade for a special Veterans Day dinner. This family is truly Patriot.

Thanksgiving

Football, family and friends. All family members are invited to bring home cooked dishes and enjoy the snow, food and football. Family members enjoy themselves. College and professional football games consume the television. When that's all over they may move some furniture to make way for a dance floor. The children and adults see who can dance the best. Leftovers are taken home for people to enjoy. At this point the Christmas tree may already be up and decorated.

Christmas Eve,

Churches have services to attend the evening of Christmas eve. On Christmas Eve Brooklyn's family gather and bring gifts for each other. They eat and go around the room and say what they are thankful for. Then they gather around Brooklyn's grandfather - Papa. He read the night before Christmas to all the children. Can you see the intense suspense on their faces as they anticipate the next line. On this day, they all wear pajamas. Each family has the same pajama print.

Christmas Day

Presents, presents, presents…….. wake up early or late, run downstairs, look at the Christmas tree, and tear open your gifts. Christ was born on this day and the parents do not let them for it. Each family stays at home and enjoys each other.

Epilogue

Use energy to make the world a better place. Redemption is motivation. Get kids educated, mentally, Cognitively, methodically, Emotionally, physically, and diabolically!! Children learn what they say and do, for example: Ashley has a prayer group around 0730am. All family members are home. This group prays and prays for family members. The family stop and bow their head for the closing prayer. This way children watch - learn - due as part of a Monday through Friday routine. Mistakes are allowed. Brooklyn tells her parents when she makes a mistake. This way the parents can correct it. They do not scold her; they teach her that mistakes are acceptable, not to be punished. Not telling is not good. We all fall, but we get up, look up, pray up, stand up and just all around Be up! It takes seven muscles to smile and forty-nine muscles to frown. Stay healthy with a smile. Teach these kids to smile. We all have that job together. Children are the experts in their destiny. They have all the tools they need. It is their leaders, teachers, and guardians that can guide them. Failure is not an option. Helping the children reach beyond the trees, clouds and the stars can be the best start. In contrast, it is instilling in them a confidence that is so great, they come to believe it. Empower the children's mind by elevating education. Again book 1 teaches how children can speak words. Book 2 illustrates how to get good nightly routes round. Book 3 shows how Nana Wynn instructs the children. Book 4 brings together the love of the child's family. Book 5 provides celebratory holidays in Brooklyn's family. But together this series depicts the plethora of ideas which teach a child how to reach beyond the trees they see, reach beyond the they live in and go for the stars.

Children know Holidays are celebrated. They may not always know the name of the exact holiday. Overall Brooklyn Love princess dresses. She was the flower girl in Grandma Sita's wedding. She sings on stage at her mom's family reunion. She enjoys movie night with her family. These are normal family festivities. Brooklyn plays with toys and her little sister. Cognitive skills start developing as soon as the child's eyes are open. It is not only a teacher or caregiver job to instruct children. It takes an entire village. All children can learn at home as well as in school. Children learn by playing with other children, from their parents in addition to caregivers. Reinforcement and repetition are the key. Brooklyn has gone to swimming classes and dance classes to help develop her skills and sharpen her tools. Nana Wynn exposed them to being a chef, a veterinarian, anything. Her parents work and take her to parks, to fish, and parties. The point is – the schools cannot and should not be expected too solely do it all. Brooklyn does not understand football, she does have an Ohio State football cheerleader outfit.

Note:

Educators and college graduates surround Brooklyn.

Nana Wynn is a retired schoolteacher, Ebone' is a schoolteacher, Granny-Sita completed Doctorial courses, Brooklyn's parents are college graduates, Brooklyn aunt Peanut and uncle graduated from college. Educators surround Brooklynn no matter who she is around. Brooklyn is always in an education environment by default.

Out of the comfort zone is the norm for this class. Out of the box thinking is logic.

Autistic children can dress and participate in classes. Sometimes parents limit what they feel the child is expected instead of seeing the limits because of exposure. All children are different. They do not have to be limited through the experience and expectations of the guardians.

Past the third grade when the student is ready to learn the teacher will appear.

Whose job is it to teach them how to or even want to focus. The eagle soars high. The eagle's child watched them soar. That is an example of expositing the child sublimely. Children who live a full life are taught by using the five senses. They see their parents go to work; they hear intelligent words they speak kindly; they know what they want to be before they reach Jr high school. It is not just in stilled within them. Teachers like Nana Wynn have brought them sublimely out of the box ready to vote, ready to color, ready to model, ready to count, ready to speak properly with a batch of homemade cognitive learning. It's up to the rest of America to help all children ages 1 to 5 get the best start possible. A child is not born lazy. A child developed that skill by not having the proper guidance. Ages one though 5 the children can exhibit how they are lively and alive. Let us go to America. Let us help them get it together. These children are not alone, they are especially ambitious. They are miraculously exposed to the possibilities of unlimited skies. They know tomatoes do not come from McDonald's but grow out of the garden. Both of Brooklyn's grandmothers have gardens. Brooklyn always helps her Nana named Regina water plants and she really enjoys it. Brooklyn is exposed to technical words instead of language that is not found in the dictionary. Church teaches the family religion, but they say grace before eating and pray before sleeping. Five golden years depict the inclusion of the real world and not the illusion of being solely taught from electronics. They are not allowed to bring an iPad into Nana Wynn home. Nana Wynn has introduced them to an extraordinary world of learning with real life experiences. The imagination of youth manifests itself into adulthood. This style of learning is not a code to be cracked but a practice to be held and uplifted in our youth. Matthew 15:18 states "Out of the mouths of babes into the minds of men." When youth is exposed to goodness, it builds up good character. It is that good character that is instilled in Brooklyn taught by Nana Wynn, demonstrated, by her parents, family, and friends, that she is surrounded by. Brooklyn and her dad do push-ups. That is not mentioned to impress – but press upon the fundamentals that you are never too young to be exposed to overachievers, little Olympians, and the like. This is the grace of education that flows into the mind that exemplifies the produced promising ideas these youth are inspired to exonerate from their mount.

Linda Berry has published a book prior to this series. The author graduated from Ashland University a B.S. in Criminal Justice Administration. While at Ashland she became the president of her sorority Delta Sigma Theta, Sorority Inc. Her master's degree is from Tiffin University in Criminal Justice/Homeland Security. She completed doctoral courses at North Central University. Linda Retired from the State of Ohio working for both the Adult Parole Authority in Cleveland, Ohio and the Department of Developmental Disabilities in Columbus, Ohio. Ms. Bery retired from the Army National Guard as a Military Police head of Operations.

Linda's volunteer work is Extensive. She gardens at the Franklin Park Conservatory in Columbus, as well as a lifetime member and Service Officer for the Veterans of Foreign War. She is a lifetime member of the VFW, American Legion, and Disenabled American Veterans. Before the pandemic Linda worked as a substitute teacher in Reynoldsburg, Ohio. She is a member of the Broad Street Presbyterian Church in Columbus, Ohio. Attends a church called the Atlanta Methodist Church in New Holland, Ohio, and cooks for the Living Waters Church in Williamsport Ohio. Linda enjoys Traveling.

She is the founder and philanthropist of Excalibur, LLC, since 1990, in Cleveland and Columbus, Ohio. Excalibur, LLC is a non-profit organization dedicated to helping at risk youth stay engaged: and employed through church activities, horticulture, helping people move and catering. The youth work all year round whenever the opportunity presents itself. Overall. Linda enjoys Traveling.

Printed in the United States
by Baker & Taylor Publisher Services